C is for Chameleon

ABC Read-With-Me Animal Babies

Written and Illustrated by:
Sarah E. Hewitt

...for Quin and Bean...

A is for

Armadillo

A baby armadillo is called a pup.

Armadillos have a very hard shell. It's almost like having their own suit of armor! When they are in danger, armadillos curl into a tight, little ball to protect their soft, furry tummies.

is
for

Buffalo

A baby buffalo is called a calf.

Baby buffaloes are born orange, but as they grow their fur darkens to a deep brown. When they grow up, buffaloes are incredibly strong and very fast. An adult buffalo can run about 40 miles per hour.

is

for

Chameleon

A baby chameleon is called a hatchling.

Chameleons change color when they're scared or angry. They have eyes that can look in two different directions to help them hunt for food. Chameleons use their long, stretchy, sticky tongues to catch bugs for a tasty breakfast.

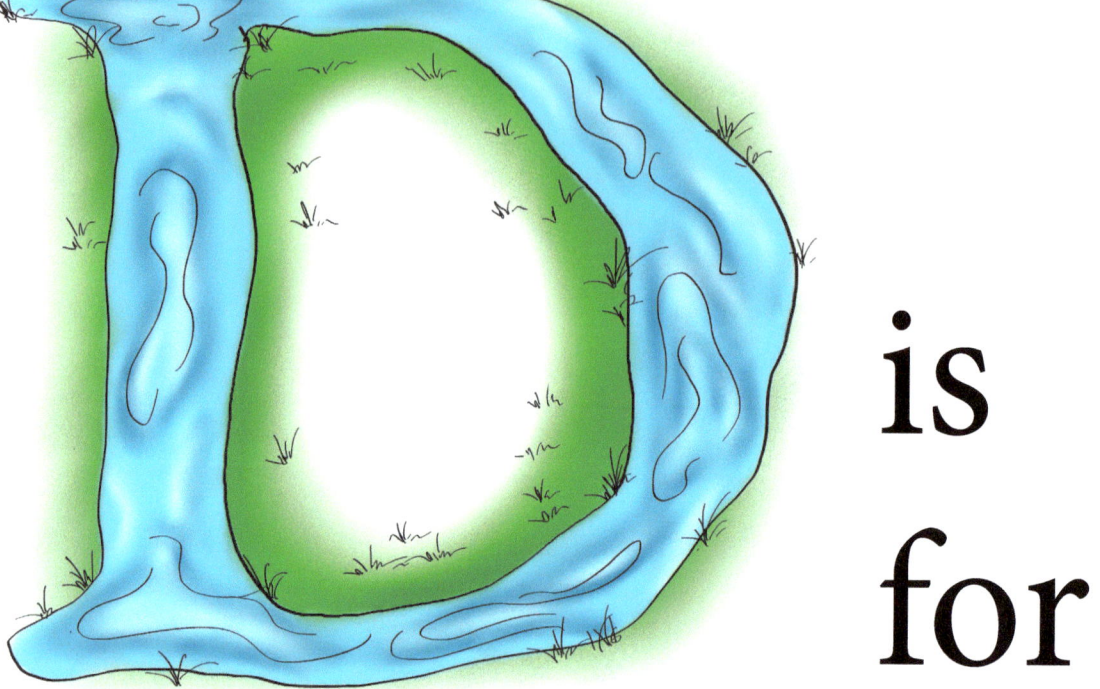

D is for

Duck

A baby duck is called a duckling.

Ducks are amazing swimmers! Their webbed feet act like swim fins to help them speed across the water and dive down deep to catch small fish and water bugs to eat. Ducks also have special waterproof feathers to help them stay dry and warm.

is for

Elephant

A baby elephant is called a calf.

Elephants have amazing memories! They say hello to each other with a "hug" by wrapping their trunks together if an elephant has been away from the herd for a long time.

 is

for

Fox

A baby fox is called a kit.

What does the fox say? Foxes make as many as 20 different sounds! Foxes are members of the dog family, but they have sharp claws like cats. Foxes also have amazing eyesight which is great for finding a midnight snack.

G is for

Giraffe

A baby giraffe is called a calf.

Sometimes it's great to be tall! Most of the time, other animals eat all of the leaves from the bottoms of the trees. Since giraffes are so tall, they only need to stretch out their long tongues to reach the sweet, new leaves and fruit in the tree tops.

is for

Hedgehog

A baby hedgehog is called a kit, a pup, or a piglet.

Hedgehogs have about 5,000 short spines on their backs to help keep them safe. They roll into a ball to protect their soft, fluffy bellies! A hungry predator will probably look somewhere else for their dinner.

is
for

Ibex

A baby ibex (EYE-beks) is called a kid.

Ibex are wild mountain goats that live in some of the highest, rocky mountains on Earth. Ibex are quick and adventurous. Their special feet make it easy to climb steep, jagged rocks to find food, play with friends, and run from danger.

is
for

Jaguar

A baby jaguar is called a cub.

Jaguars can see six times better than people. With eyes like night-vision goggles, jaguars are amazing hunters! They also have the strongest jaws and teeth of any type of big cat, so they can carry their dinner up into a tree to have a tasty meal all to themselves.

is

for

Koala

A baby koala is called a joey.

When they're born, a joey is the size of a jellybean. They crawl into their mother's pouch to stay warm and safe until they've grown big and strong enough to come out into the world. Then, the joeys will piggy-back ride on their mother until they're old enough to go out on their own.

is

for

Lemur

A baby lemur is called a pup.

Male lemurs battle for power, girlfriends, and territory by trying to out-stink each other! They rub their very smelly, oily secretions all over their tails, wave them in the air, and dance to show who is stronger.

is for

Moose

A baby moose is called a calf.

Moose may look cute and cuddly, but they are actually very dangerous! When they're grown, moose can be as tall as a grown man and weigh more than a car! When moose grow up, they grow huge antlers that reach about six feet across!

 is for

Narwhal

A baby narwhal is called a calf.

Narwhals are very hard to study because they're shy creatures that love to hide deep in the freezing waters of the Arctic Ocean. Scientists don't know a lot about narwhals, or why they have the long, spiral, "unicorn" tusk coming out of their heads!

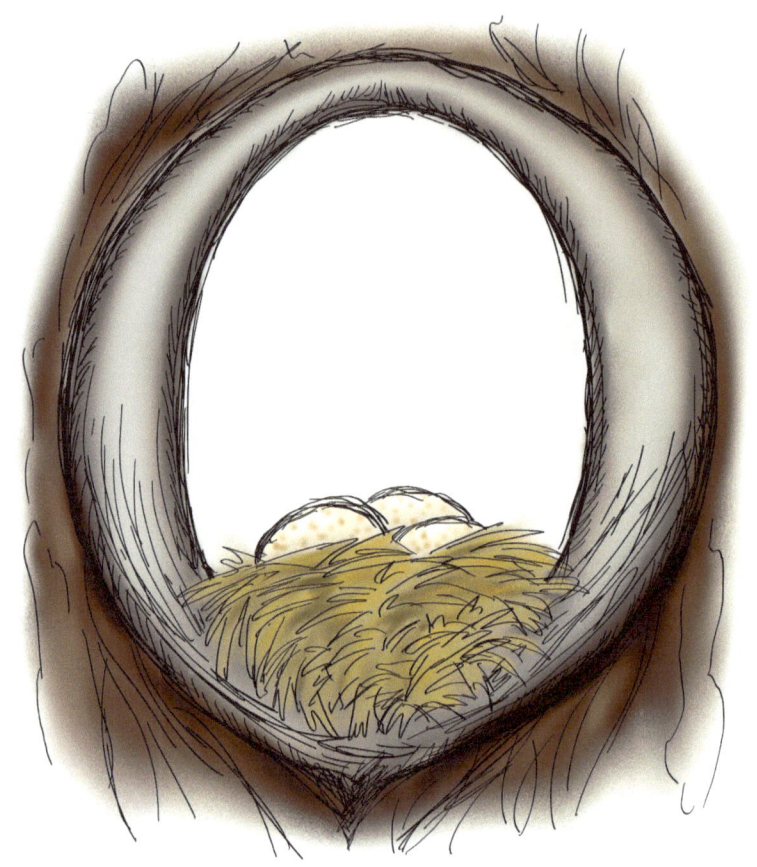 is for

Owl

A baby owl is called an owlet.

Owls have huge eyes that help them see at night. They do have a problem, though. Owls' eyes are shaped like long tubes, almost like binoculars, so owls have to move their heads up and down and side-to-side in order to see what's around them.

is for

Platypus

A baby platypus doesn't have a special name but is sometimes called a platypup.

Platypuses have a rubbery bill and webbed feet like a duck; a wide, flat tail like a beaver; and slick, dark fur like an otter. Platypuses are incredible swimmers and are one of the only mammals to lay eggs!

is for

Quail

A baby quail is called a chick.

Quail have a funny-looking group of feathers on top of their head that is shaped like a question mark; these feathers are called a top-knot. Even though quail can fly, they would rather run through the bushes and tall grass to find seeds, bugs, and other food to eat.

Rhino

A baby rhino is called a calf.

Rhinos grow long horns on the top of their noses that help protect them from danger. A rhino's best friend is the oxpecker, a bird who sits on the rhino's back and eats the creepy, crawly bugs that crawl all over the rhino's skin.

is
for

Sloth

A baby sloth is called a pup.

Sloths are the world's slowest animal. They sleep between 15 and 20 hours every day! They spend most of their lives hanging upside-down, eating leaves, and sleeping the day away.

is

for

Tortoise

A baby tortoise is called a hatchling.

When they hatch, tortoises are very, very tiny. Some are as small as a quarter! Tortoises can grow up to four feet long and weigh almost 450 pounds! Tortoises live an extremely long time. The oldest tortoise was believed to be about 250 years old!

is
for

Uinta Chipmunk

A baby Uinta (you-IN-tuh) Chipmunk is called a
pup, a kit or a cub.

Uinta Chipmunks carry food to their burrows in special pouches
in their cheeks. In their burrows, the chipmunks store nuts,
berries, seeds, and other food to eat in the winter and to share with
their friends and family.

 is

for

Vole

A baby vole is called a pup.

Voles are sometimes called field mice or meadow mice. They are extremely good at digging and burrowing. They love to eat the roots of vegetable plants and flowers, which can sometimes cause a problem for people with gardens.

is
for

Wolverine

A baby wolverine is called a kit.

Wolverines are related to weasels and skunks. Like their relatives, wolverines can't see very well. In order to find food, they have to use their super-hearing and sensitive noses. Wolverines sometimes have to walk more than 20 miles in one day just for a snack!

is
for

Xenops

A baby xenops (ZEN-ops) is called a chick.

Ants and their larvae make a tasty treat for a hungry xenops! In order to find something to munch on, xenops have to use their strong beaks to pound holes into old, dead trees where the ants make their homes.

is

for

Yak

A baby yak is called a calf.

Yaks live in the highest mountains on Earth! Yaks are able to survive in the freezing, windy mountains because of their extremely thick, warm fur. Huge, wide hooves act like snowshoes to help yaks stay safely on top of the snow so they don't get stuck in a snow drift!

is

for

Zebra

A baby zebra is called a foal.

Male baby zebras are called colts and females are called fillies.

Sometimes it's good to blend in! Black and white stripes help protect zebras from predators. Their striped pattern makes it very difficult for a hungry lion or cheetah to pick out one zebra from the rest of the herd.

www.ingramcontent.com/pod-product-compliance
Lightning Source LLC
Chambersburg PA
CBHW041509280526
45792CB00004B/1195